Author's Note

This workbook is not centered on morality, cultural beliefs, cultural norms, or religion. It is not written as a challenge to those who enjoy recreational sexuality or nontraditional sexuality, either casually or as a lifestyle. As a mental health and addiction professional, it is not my job to judge such behaviors in any way. Instead, I have written this book to help people whose sexual fantasies and activities have run amok to the point where they've become a driving life force, overriding their personal goals, beliefs, and lifestyle. In other words, this book is written for those whose involvement with objectified, non-intimate sexuality consistently and persistently distracts them from their larger personal goals.

Although there are many views about whether things like pornography, virtual sex, casual/anonymous sex, and nontraditional sex are right or wrong, good or bad, moral or immoral, it is not the intent of this book to define or address these issues in any meaningful way. I support every adult in his or her right to engage in any solo or mutually consensual (and legal) sexual activity or experience that provides pleasure, satisfaction, and fulfillment. I do not believe that anyone, therapist or not, has the right to judge what turns someone on or how a person pursues sexual activity, as long as that person's choices do not violate the intrinsic rights and safety of self or others.

My primary goal here is to assist people who struggle with compulsive and addictive sexual behaviors by helping them to identify their problem as the chronic emotional disorder it is, and to then understand that their problem can be put into remission with proper care and direction—just like alcoholism, compulsive gambling, eating disorders, and drug addiction. In a nutshell, I want those who are suffering from sexual addiction to know that their sexual concerns can be addressed without shame or moral/cultural/religious bias. I also seek to offer direction and insight to therapists who may be unfamiliar with the treatment of sexually addicted clients. Most of all, I want to offer sex addicts hope, letting them know that long-term change and healing are possible to anyone willing to invest in the process of recovery.

—Robert Weiss LCSW, CSAT-S

How to Get the Most Out of This Workbook

This workbook is built on research-based addiction treatment methods and more than twenty years of professional experience as a sex addiction treatment specialist. In other words, a whole lot of scientific knowledge and clinical experience has gone into this manual. In fact, over the years and in various forms the 24 updated and highly refined exercises included herein have helped thousands of men and women heal from sex, porn, and/or love addiction.

It is my hope that you will not use this workbook as a standalone resource in your process of healing, as it is written and intended for use in conjunction with my deeper and more informative full-length book, *Sex Addiction 101: A Basic Guide to Healing from Sex, Love, and Porn Addiction*. That more traditional book and this workbook are meant complement one another. The traditional book provides in-depth information about the nature, causes, and treatment of sexual addiction, and I suggest that you read it first, as that is where you will find the information, direction, and illustrative stories that underlie the concrete exercises outlined in this workbook. Meanwhile, this workbook provides tasks and reflective questions designed to help you establish and maintain sexual sobriety, and to live a more serene and fulfilling life.

> NOTE: This workbook is available in both print and digital editions. If you choose the print version, space is provided in which you can complete the exercises. If you opt for an eBook, you will need to have your laptop or a notebook handy, as you will be doing a fair amount of writing. Neither method is better than the other. Some people like to do things the old-fashioned way; others are deeply digital in their methodology. Whatever format works best for you, have at it.

To achieve an optimal outcome, I strongly advise you to share your in-depth responses to the exercises in this workbook with others who understand sexual addiction and support your recovery—therapists, 12-step sponsors, friends in recovery, trusted clergy, and the like—as these individuals can provide you with a sounding board, feedback, and emotional support. When you share your work with knowledgeable, compassionate, and supportive people in this way, you are much less likely to miss things and to remain in denial about certain aspects of your addiction. More importantly, many of the exercises are likely to create strong and very uncomfortable feelings—dredging up the past has a way of doing that—and who better to help you process these emotions (without acting out) than your recovery support network? At the very least, these folks can reel you in if/when you start to beat yourself up about your past.

If you are married or in some other committed long-term relationship, I do not recommend sharing the work you do in this book with your partner. The exercises in this workbook are meant to help you with your sexual and emotional challenges. They are not focused on your spouse or your relationship. Yes, there is a time and place for transparency and disclosure as a part of relationship healing, but this should not occur without guidance and support from an experienced couple's therapist, preferably one who is familiar with and trained to handle sexual addiction issues. So don't leave this workbook on your desk, or the dining room table, or anyplace else where your understandably curious partner might easily access it. And please don't spontaneously decide to share your work with your significant other, even if you feel really good about the work you're doing. No matter how well intentioned you are, premature, unsupervised disclosures nearly always cause more harm than healing.

That said, it is perfectly OK to let your spouse know that you have purchased this workbook and you are actively completing the exercises as part of your sexual recovery. But make it clear that this workbook is designed to benefit you and your sexual sobriety, not your mate or your relationship. If your significant other is curious and really wants to know what you're doing, the best thing you can do is to suggest that he or she read this workbook's companion volume, *Sex Addiction 101: A Basic Guide to Healing from Sex, Porn, and Love Addiction*. You might also suggest that the two of you enter into couples counseling, which lets you talk about your issues and the work you are doing in a safe and controlled setting, where your and your partner's emotions can be healthfully processed and resolved.

For simplicity and clarity, the exercises in this workbook are divided into five basic sections, each designed to walk you through a different phase of healing.

- Section one gets you started on the pathway to recovery, helping you develop a personalized definition of and plan for sexual sobriety.
- Section two helps you better understand the various facets and nuances of your addiction.
- Section three focuses on relapse prevention, in particular the development of coping skills that can help you stay sober no matter what.
- Section four starts you on the "next step" of healing by identifying and addressing the underlying issues that drive your addictive behavior.
- Section five addresses life in sobriety, including dating and developing a happier, more well-rounded life.

Even though writing down some information in a workbook may initially seem like a humdrum endeavor, I can assure you that in this instance it is not. The issues you are writing about and the feelings this work will evoke are deep and meaningful. As such, it is imperative that you take breaks when needed—going for walks, talking with supportive friends, taking naps, hitting the gym, and doing whatever else it is that helps you feel less stressed (except for sexual acting out). The goal is not to finish this workbook in record time, it's to engage in careful thought and analysis, taking time to feel whatever it is that you need to feel. So take as much time as you need. However, you should not procrastinate simply because the exercises in this book and the emotions they evoke are not always fun and uplifting.

> NOTE: If you find that the exercises in this workbook cause you to feel extreme stress, anxiety, or depression (perhaps to the point of not wanting to live), put the book down and *seek professional assistance immediately*. After all, this book is meant to help you, not to punish you or make you miserable. Hopefully, at a later date when your emotional discomfort has passed, you'll be able to return to these exercises in a better frame of mind, resuming your recovery from sexual addiction.

In closing, I strongly suggest, no matter where you are in your personal healing journey, that you work the exercises in the order presented. Even if you've already spent valuable time looking at your past, you are likely to uncover new and important issues by repeating this effort. And, once again, I encourage you to share your work with others who understand sexual addiction and support your recovery. You will get much more bang for your buck if you do, and you will find it much easier to remain sexually sober.

Section One: Getting Started

The journey of a thousand miles begins with one step.
—Lao Tzu

Exercise 1: Sexual Addiction Self-Screening Quiz

If you are uncertain as to whether you might be a sex addict, the following quiz is designed to give you some clarity. This test is similar to the twenty-question quiz that Alcoholics Anonymous offers to help people decide if they are alcoholic. A scoring key can be found at the end of the test.

Please answer yes or no to the following 15 questions. In doing so, you should consider your entire sexual history, not just recent events. In other words, if you were abusing porn three years ago but lately your issue has been hookup apps, you should still take your past porn use into account.

1. Do you find that sexual fantasy, seeking sex, and having sex have become more important in your life than other things that you need (and probably want) to focus on, such as work, family, and non-sexual hobbies?

   ○ Yes ○ No

2. Do you ever regret amount of the time you spend fantasizing about, searching for, and engaging in sex?

   ○ Yes ○ No

3. Have you promised yourself that you will stop visiting certain sexual websites, using porn, using certain sexual apps, or engaging in certain real world sexual activities, only to find yourself back there again anyway?

   ○ Yes ○ No

4. If you are in a committed relationship, do you repeatedly find yourself engaging in secretive sexual affairs or casual sexual activities?

   ○ Yes ○ No

5. Do you find yourself habitually going online, looking for sex and "losing yourself" for long periods of time, even when your clear intention was to only be online for a few minutes?

   ○ Yes ○ No

6. Has your obsessive focus on finding and having sex reduced your ability to focus on and "be present" with your romantic partner, family, friends, spirituality, work, school, recreational activities, and/or other important aspects of life?
    ○ Yes ○ No

7. Do you lie and keep secrets from those close to you about your sexual and/or romantic pursuits and behaviors?
    ○ Yes ○ No

8. Has your obsessive focus on finding and having sex created negative consequences in your life, such as ruined relationships, trouble at work or in school, depression, isolation, anxiety, loss of interest in previously enjoyable activities, financial woes, legal issues, declining physical health, etc.?
    ○ Yes ○ No

9. Do you cover up and hide aspects of your sexual life, hoping to avoid consequences that might occur if you are discovered or found out?
    ○ Yes ○ No

10. If you are in a committed relationship, would your partner say (if he or she knew everything) that your sexual activity violates relationship boundaries and his or her trust?
    ○ Yes ○ No

11. Has your sexual and/or romantic behavior caused you to lose anyone or anything important in your life—romantic relationships, family, career, school, money, self-esteem, community standing, etc.?
    ○ Yes ○ No

12. Have you ever been arrested, formally warned, or otherwise reprimanded because of your sexual behavior?
    ○ Yes ○ No

13. Do you view, download, share, or distribute illegal sexual imagery or engage in illegal sexual activity (exhibitionism, voyeurism, prostitution, illegal pornography, etc.)?
    ○ Yes ○ No

14. Has your partner, your family, your employer, or a friend ever complained or expressed concern about the nature and/or the extent of your sexual activity?
    ○ Yes ○ No

15. Do you become defensive, angry, or extremely ashamed when asked to look at, give up, or curtail your sexual activities?
    ○ Yes ○ No

SCORING: If you did not answer yes to any of these questions, you are probably not a sex addict. If you answered yes to one or two questions, you are at risk for sexual addiction. If you answered yes to three or more questions, there is a definite possibility that you are sexually addicted.

NOTE: An affirmative answer to question 13, regarding illegal sexual activity, is *always* a problem, even if you're not a sex addict. If you answered yes to that question, you should absolutely seek confidential advice from a professional counselor who is skilled in handling such issues. However, if/when you do this, be aware of the fact that licensed psychotherapists have mandated reporting requirements (that vary from state to state) when it comes to illegal sexual behaviors. You need to find out what these requirements are before you talk in detail about your behavior.

Exercise 2: Are You *Really* a Sex Addict?

Sex addicts, especially those new to the process of recovery, are typically in denial about their problem, even after they've answered yes to the majority of the questions in Exercise 1. They just find it hard to accept that they truly are sexually addicted, and that they're going to have to make some major changes or things are going to completely fall apart (even worse than they already have).

Generally speaking, there are three primary criteria for sexual addiction:

1) Preoccupation to the point of obsession with sexual fantasies and behaviors, with the preoccupation lasting six months or longer
2) Loss of control over these sexual fantasies and behaviors, typically evidenced by failed attempts to quit or cut back
3) Negative life consequences related to these out-of-control sexual fantasies and behaviors—relationship trouble, issues at work or in school, declining physical health, depression, anxiety, diminished self-esteem, isolation, financial woes, loss of interest in previously enjoyable activities, legal trouble, etc.

Other common signs and symptoms of sexual addiction include: consistent sexual objectification of self and/or others, tolerance and escalation, withdrawal, and denial. However, these are not necessary when assessing for and identifying sexual addiction.

The following exercise is designed to help you to see the true nature of your addiction by looking at the three primary sex addiction criteria.

List examples of your preoccupation/obsession with sex.

Example: *Before I even get out of bed, I grab my iPhone and check to see if anyone looked at or contacted me on one of my hookup app profiles.*

_____

_____

_____

_____

_____

_____

_____

_____

_____

_____

Write a few lines about how your preoccupation/obsession with sex makes you feel (shameful, weak, hopeless, embarrassed, etc.), and why.

_____

_____

_____

_____

_____

List any attempts you've made to either quit or curtail your sexual behaviors. Note the approximate length of your success.

Example: *After getting in trouble at work for misusing my laptop, I swore off of porn forever. Three days later I borrowed a friend's laptop to cruise for porn.*

_____

_____

_____

_____

_____

_____

_____

_____

_____

_____

Why do you think you have been unable to successfully curtail these sexual behaviors?

_____

_____

_____

_____

_____

List any negative life consequences you've experienced related to your sexual behaviors.

Example: *A woman I loved and wanted to marry dumped me when she found out I was hooking up with dozens of other women every month.*

_____

_____

_____

_____

_____

_____

_____

_____

_____

Have these negative consequences affected your sexual behavior patterns? If so, in what ways? And how do you feel about that?

_____

_____

_____

_____

_____

Exercise 3: Powerlessness and Unmanageability

Step 1 for 12-Step Sexual Recovery

"We admitted we were powerless over sex, and that our lives had become unmanageable."

In some ways, this exercise covers the same basic ground as Exercises 1 and 2, but it does so in 12-step recovery program language, where addiction is defined by "powerlessness" and "unmanageability." In fact, the initial work in all 12-step recovery programs involves an admission that you are powerless over your addiction and your addiction has caused your life to become unmanageable.

- **Powerless** means you have lost control over your sexual behaviors. You engage in these behaviors compulsively, even when you say you don't want to. And you have no ability to stop your sexual behaviors once you've started (at least not until after sex and orgasm). Put simply, powerlessness means that despite the promises you've made to yourself and/or others that you are going to stop your sexual acting out, you find yourself right back at it.
- **Unmanageable** speaks primarily to the consequences of your compulsive sexual behaviors, both direct (obviously connected) and indirect (less obviously connected). Many sex addicts have relationship troubles, STDs, reprimands at work, and even arrests that are very obviously connected to their out-of-control sexual behaviors. Less obvious consequences may include depression, anxiety, feeling worn out, forgetting to pay bills, eating poorly, loss of interest in previously enjoyable activities, etc. Any and all of these issues, both direct and indirect, are examples of unmanageability.

List examples of your powerlessness over your sexual behaviors. Use the following format: "Even though I (list a particular consequence), I continued to (list a particular addictive sexual activity)."

Example: *Even though I got a written warning at work for misusing my company issued phone, I continued to use hookup apps on it.*

_____

_____

_____

_____

_____

_____

_____

_____

_____

List examples of unmanageability (problems and consequences) related to your sexual behaviors.

Example: *I was fired from my job for repeatedly taking long lunches, mostly because I was getting erotic massages and lap dances.*

_____

_____

_____

_____

_____

_____

_____

_____

_____

Do you feel that you are powerless over some of your sexual behaviors and, as a result, that parts of your life have become unmanageable? If so, how do you feel about that?

_____

_____

_____

_____

_____

Exercise 4: Creating Your Sexual Sobriety Plan

Many sex addicts who are new to the healing process worry that sexual sobriety requires total and permanent sexual abstinence (as with substance abuse recovery). Happily, that is not the case. Instead, sex addicts create a personalized definition of sexual sobriety by delineating the sexual behaviors that do and do not compromise and/or destroy their values, life circumstances, and relationships. Then they agree to avoid their problematic sexual behaviors in the future. As long as their sexual behaviors do not violate these highly individualized boundaries, they are sexually sober.

Because the definition of sexual sobriety takes into account each person's values, beliefs, goals, and life history, sexual sobriety looks different for every addict. For instance, sexual sobriety for a 22-year-old unpartnered gay man will probably not match sexual sobriety for a straight 47-year-old married father of three. The goal is not conformity. Instead, the goal is a non-compulsive, non-secretive, non-shaming sexual life.

Typically, the process of defining your sexual sobriety begins with a list of goals. A few commonly stated goals are:

- I no longer want to cheat on or keep secrets from my spouse.
- I don't want to worry about catching and/or transmitting STDs anymore.
- I want to date and feel connected and cared about, instead of just getting off.
- I don't want to "lose myself" to pornography and hookup apps anymore, forgetting about (or ignoring) other, more important parts of my life.
- I don't want to ever again get reprimanded, fired, approached by security, or arrested regarding my sexual behavior.
- I want an intimate, caring, honest, and emotionally engaged relationship with my partner.

Many people will also list less tangible goals like "being a better person" and "living my life with integrity," and that is fine, as long as concrete, sex-specific goals are also mentioned, such as quitting problematic behaviors, mending broken relationships, and avoiding future consequences.

Once your goals are clearly stated, you can move forward with the creation of your personalized sexual boundary plan. These plans, created to support your goals for recovery, are broken into inner, middle, and outer boundaries as follows:

The Inner Boundary

This is your bottom line definition of sexual sobriety. Here you list the specific sexual behaviors (not thoughts or fantasies) that are causing problems in your life and you therefore need to stop. In other words, your inner boundary lists the damaging and troublesome acts that are ruining your life. A few common inner boundary behaviors are as follows:

- Paying for sex and/or sensual massage
- Hooking up for casual and/or anonymous sex
- Going online for porn or webcam sex
- Masturbating to porn
- Having affairs

The Middle Boundary

This boundary lists warning signs and slippery situations that might lead you back to inner boundary behaviors. Here you list the people, places, thoughts, fantasies, events, and experiences that might trigger your desire to act out sexually. In addition to obvious potential triggers—logging on to the Internet, driving through a neighborhood where prostitutes hang out, downloading a hookup app—this list should include things that might indirectly trigger a desire to act out—working long hours, keeping secrets, worrying about finances. A few common middle boundary items are as follows:

- Skipping therapy and/or a support group meeting
- Lying (about anything), especially to a loved one
- Feeling hungry, angry, anxious, lonely, bored, tired, etc.
- Fighting and/or arguing, especially with loved ones and/or authority figures
- Unstructured time alone

The Outer Boundary

This boundary lists healthy behaviors and activities that can and hopefully will lead you toward your life goals, including but not even remotely limited to having a healthy, non-destructive sex life. These healthy pleasures are what you can turn to as a replacement for sexual acting out. Outer boundary activities may be immediate and concrete, such as "working on the house," or long-term and less tangible, such as "redefining my career goals." In all cases, the list should reflect a healthy combination of work, recovery, and play. A few common outer boundary behaviors are as follows:

- Spend more time with my family, especially my kids.
- Reconnect with old friends.
- Rekindle an old hobby (or develop a new one).
- Get in shape, or at least engage in more physical activities.
- Do volunteer work and become more active in my community.

When crafting a sexual boundary plan, one potentially tricky area is masturbation. For many sex addicts, masturbation is an integral part of the addictive cycle, escalating the fantasies that produce the "high" of sexual addiction. In such cases, masturbation is either a slippery but still sober middle boundary behavior or a bottom line inner boundary behavior. For other sex addicts, masturbation may actually aid recovery, encouraging appropriate intimacy and contributing to an overall sense of sexual health and wellbeing. Given the confusion about masturbation and where to place it within one's sexual boundary plan, recovering sex addicts should always discuss the issue with their therapist or some other accountability partner, preferably erring on the side of caution.

Each sexual boundary plan starts with a listing of goals (reasons you're seeking change). Please list your goals for sexual recovery.

Example: *I don't want to cheat on my spouse ever again.*

_____

_____

_____

_____

_____

Your inner boundary lists the bottom line sexual behaviors that you need to stop. These are the activities (not thoughts) that are causing problems in your life. Please list here all of the sexual behaviors that drove you into recovery—the activities that you need to stop and stop now.

Example: *Looking at and masturbating to pornography (of any kind).*

_____

_____

_____

_____

_____

Your middle boundary lists warning signs and slippery situations that might lead you back to inner boundary activities. Please list here the people, places, thoughts, fantasies, events, and experiences that might either directly or indirectly spark your desire to act out sexually.

Example: *Finding myself alone for long stretches of time with nothing specific to do.*

_____

_____

_____

_____

_____

Your outer boundary lists healthy behaviors and activities that can lead you toward your short and long-term life goals, including but not even remotely limited to having a healthy, nondestructive, and emotionally satisfying sex life. Please list here the healthy behaviors you can turn to as a replacement for your sexual acting out.

Example: *I want to spend more time playing games and having fun with friends and family, especially my kids.*

_____

_____

_____

_____

_____

Section Two: Understanding Your Addiction

Ignorance is the curse of God; knowledge is the wing wherewith we fly to heaven.
—William Shakespeare

Exercise 5: Denial

Unlike healthy people who use past mistakes and their feelings about those mistakes to guide future decisions and behaviors, sex addicts tend to deny and defend against the problematic nature of their choices, rationalizing and justifying behaviors that pretty much anyone else could and would readily identify as troubling, compulsive, and maybe even dangerous. In short, sex addicts find ways to ignore the seriousness of their sexual acting out so they can continue with those behaviors. Unfortunately, this willful ignorance—this denial—can go on for years.

With sexual addiction, denial can take many forms. The most common are listed below.

Blame/Externalization

- My spouse never wants to try anything new in bed. Otherwise, I wouldn't be looking for satisfaction elsewhere.
- I can't help it if other people come on to me.
- My partner has gained a lot of weight since we got married, and that's unattractive to me.

Entitlement

- I earn all the money for my family and nobody appreciates that, so I look at porn for a few hours here and there as my reward.
- I'm lonely and bored, and that's just not the way that life is supposed to be.
- I deserve to have some fun.

Justification

- If I was in a relationship I'd be having sex all the time, so why can't I have sex all the time when I'm single?
- I need to do this to reduce my tension and anxiety.
- Everybody else can look at porn, so why can't I?

Minimization

- I'll only do this one more time.
- What my spouse doesn't know can't hurt him/her.
- All I'm doing is chatting on webcam. It's not like I'm actually cheating.

Rationalization

- I see prostitutes, but I'm nice to them. I pay them what they want and even give them a little extra. I'm clean and a good lover, too, and that's a nice treat for them.
- Nobody will find out, so what I'm doing is not a big deal.
- Everybody looks at porn and plays around with hookup apps. That's just life in the modern world.

Victim Mentality

- I was sexually abused as a kid, so this behavior is expected.
- Everybody wants so much from me. I just feel overwhelmed and at the mercy of everyone in my life. And my only relief, the only time I feel in control, is when I'm being sexual.
- Look how much I am giving to my family, my friends, my work. What about me? When is it my turn?

As a sex addict, you almost certainly engage in extensive denial. The following exercise will help you to see the ways in which your denial facilitates your addiction.

List examples for each form of denial you've used to support your sexual behaviors.

Blame/Externalization

Example: *My mate ignores my sexual needs, so my cheating is his/her fault, not mine.*

_____

_____

_____

Entitlement

Example: *I work hard and I provide for my family, so I deserve a little reward.*

_____

_____

_____

Justification

Example: *My life is stressful, and a little bit of casual sex is a great way to relax.*

_____

_____

_____

Minimization

Example: *I'm only masturbating on webcams. It's not like I'm having sex with a real person.*

_____

_____

_____

Rationalization

Example: *Some guys grab a couple of beers after work. I get a massage. What's the difference?*

_____

_____

_____

Victim Mentality

Example: *My partner doesn't love me or want to have sex with me. So what am I supposed to do?*

_____

_____

_____

Write a few lines about the responses given above, specifically addressing what you learned about your denial and how you feel about this insight.

_____

_____

_____

_____

_____

If you have a therapist, a 12-step sexual recovery sponsor, or supportive friends in recovery, try reading your examples of denial to one or more of them. If you are able to do this, what did these rationalizations sound like out loud in the presence of another person? What responses did you get?

_____

_____

_____

_____

_____

Exercise 6: Tolerance and Escalation

Addicts of all types experience an increasing tolerance to the mood-altering effects of their behavior. As a result, they must, over time, use more of or a more intense version of their addiction if they wish to achieve and maintain the desired neurochemical high. As an example, consider drug abuse. Almost nobody shoots heroin right out of the gate. Instead, drug addicts ease into things by drinking alcohol, smoking marijuana, or abusing a prescription medication. Then, as time passes, their tolerance increases and, in response, their habits escalate. Before they know it, they're in a back alley with a needle in their arm.

Sex addicts escalate their behavior in similar fashion. For instance, occasionally viewing and masturbating to generic (i.e., vanilla) online porn is typically regarded as an enjoyable and relatively innocuous activity, akin to drinking a beer or inhaling a few puffs of marijuana. For some people, however, harmless recreation escalates into an all-consuming activity, pushing the user away from relationships, family, work, hobbies, and other life-affirming activities. Hours and sometimes even days are lost to digital sexual intensity. Eventually, the user is looking at and being turned on by increasingly more intense sexual imagery and/or engaging in other sexual activities (webcam sex, casual sex, anonymous sex, etc.)

As mentioned above, there are two ways in which sexual addiction escalates. One involves increased time devoted to the addiction. The other involves increased intensity. It is likely that you experienced both—losing immense amounts of time and engaging in behaviors that would have seemed outrageous when you started. This exercise will help you see the ways in which your addiction has escalated, and how this has affected you.

List examples of time-related escalation you've experienced with your addiction.

Example: *In the beginning, I would use a hookup app once or twice a week at most, usually on a Friday or a Saturday if/when I didn't have a date. Now I'm on multiple apps nonstop, 24/7/365. I even check them in the middle of the night sometimes.*

_____

_____

_____

_____

_____

_____

_____

_____

_____

_____

List examples of intensity-related escalation you've experienced with your addiction.

Example: *In the beginning, I was totally turned on by soft-core porn. But as my addiction has progressed I've been looking at harder stuff, including all sorts of kinky stuff that would have grossed me out when I started.*

_____

_____

_____

_____

_____

_____

_____

_____

_____

Do you find yourself engaging in behaviors today that surprise you or that violate your personal code of ethics? If so, what are they, and how do you feel about that?

_____

_____

_____

_____

_____

Exercise 7: Cross and Co-Occurring Addictions

Secondary addictions and compulsions are common among sex addicts (and other types of addicts, too). In this exercise we are focused on two types of secondary addictions: cross-addictions and co-occurring addictions.

- **Cross addiction** occurs when addicts switch from one problem behavior/substance to another. For example, when a cross-addicted sex addict/alcoholic is not behaving in sexually compulsive ways, he or she is probably drinking alcoholically, and when the addict is not drinking, he or she is probably acting out sexually.
- **Co-occurring addiction** occurs when addicts use multiple addictive behaviors/substances simultaneously. For example, many sex addicts are co-addicted to both sex and stimulant drugs such as cocaine and methamphetamine. If these individuals are getting high, they are almost certainly chasing sex too, and if they are chasing sex, they are probably also getting high.

Alcohol, used as both a disinhibitor and as a way to feel better about tolerating uncomfortable sexual behavior choices, is among the most common secondary drugs of choice for sex addicts. Stimulant drugs (cocaine, meth) are also commonly abused in conjunction with sex. Additionally, many of the men and women with a co-occurring sex and stimulant addiction abuse benzodiazepines (Valium, Ativan, Xanax, and the like), alcohol, and/or over-the-counter cold medicines as a way to "come down" and get some sleep when the party is finally over. Erection enhancers like Viagra, Levitra, and Cialis are also commonly abused in conjunction with sexual addiction.

As my longtime friend and colleague Pat Carnes notes in his highly regarded article, "Bargains with Chaos: Sex Addicts and Addiction Interaction Disorder," secondary addictions and compulsions typically manifest in one of eleven basic ways:

1. **Alternating Cycles**: Switching back and forth from one addiction to another, often for years on end (i.e., flipping between binge drinking and sexual acting out)
2. **Combining**: Combining various addictive substances/behaviors to create the perfect high (i.e., mixing meth with porn and then cybersex)

3. **Cross-Tolerance**: Using one addiction as a way to tolerate another (i.e., getting drunk or smoking cigarettes to self-soothe shame about sexual behaviors)

4. **Disinhibiting**: Using one addiction to reduce inhibitions related to a second addiction (i.e., getting high before having sex with a stranger or a prostitute)

5. **Fusing**: Using one addiction to amplify another (i.e., using cocaine or methamphetamine to heighten the pleasure of orgasm)

6. **Inhibiting**: Viewing one addiction as the lesser of two evils (i.e., smoking cigarettes instead of looking at porn all night)

7. **Masking**: Using one addiction to hide another (i.e., going to AA for alcoholism but never looking at compulsive sexual activity)

8. **Numbing**: Using one addiction to numb the shame of another (i.e., getting drunk or high after cheating on your spouse)

9. **Replacement**: Replacing one addiction with another (i.e., cutting down on the use of hookup apps by gambling for hours on end)

10. **Rituals**: Incorporating one addiction into the ritual phase of another (i.e., buying cocaine or methamphetamine before beginning the search for a prostitute)

11. **Withdrawal Mediation**: Using one addiction to stop another (i.e., shopping compulsively as a way to stay out of sex clubs)

List any and all potentially addictive substances that you have used in your lifetime, noting how often you currently use them. Highlight or otherwise note any substances that you have consistently used in conjunction with sexual behaviors. (Do not ignore prescription meds like Viagra, Xanax, and the like.)

Example: *Marijuana. I started when I was 14. I get high several times per week, if not daily. Before I head out to have sex with someone I've met on a hookup app, I smoke some dope to relax.*

_____

_____

_____

_____

_____

_____

_____

_____

_____

_____

List any (nonsexual) addictive/compulsive behaviors (binge eating, compulsive gambling, compulsive spending, etc.) you have used in your lifetime, noting how often you currently engage in these behaviors. Highlight or otherwise note any behaviors you have consistently used in conjunction with sexual behaviors (including use as a way to avoid feeling shame about your sex life).

Example: _Binge eating. This started in my late teens. I almost always do this after I act out sexually. For instance, after I see a prostitute I'll buy a half-gallon of ice cream and eat the whole thing, trying to make myself feel better._

_____

_____

_____

_____

_____

_____

_____

_____

_____

_____

Do you feel that you might have (or that you could eventually develop) a cross or co-occurring addiction? If so, what is it, and what makes you think it might be a problem? And how do you feel about this revelation?

_____

_____

_____

_____

_____

What, if anything, are you willing to do to address this secondary issue (i.e., go to therapy, attend a 12-step group, talk to a friend or family member, etc.)?

_____

_____

_____

_____

_____

Exercise 8: Triggers

Sex addiction triggers are thoughts and feelings that induce the strong desire—the craving—to engage in addictive sexual fantasies and behaviors. There are two primary types of triggers: internal and external.

- **Internal triggers** typically involve some type of emotional discomfort—depression, shame, anxiety, anger, fear, guilt, remorse, boredom, etc. For instance, if/when a married sex addict's spouse is away for a few days (or even a few hours), he or she might feel lonely, and this emotional discomfort might trigger a desire to act out sexually.
- **External triggers** are people, places, things, and/or events. For instance, if/when a sex addict sees an old affair partner; he or she might be triggered to act out sexually.

Sex addicts must also deal with intertwined triggers (triggers that are both internal and external). For instance, if/when a sex addict argues with his or her spouse or has a bad day at work (an external trigger) he or she is likely to experience emotional discomfort (an internal trigger), with both triggers causing a desire to act out sexually. And this desire may be exacerbated by visual triggers that remind the addict of his or her addiction (such as driving past strip clubs and prostitutes).

> NOTE: Not all triggers are negative in nature. For example, material successes and positive emotions will often evoke a desire to celebrate, and thus a desire to act out sexually.

In truth, almost anything can be a trigger. Even past memories can be triggers. For instance, if your boss looks at one of your co-workers crossly, this might remind you of your alcoholic father and the way he used to hit and yell at your brother, thereby creating various forms of emotional discomfort for you in the current moment—fear, anger, shame, etc. This emotional discomfort can then become a trigger for your sexual addiction, even though your boss's cross expression has nothing at all to do with you.

A few of the more common *internal triggers* for sexual acting out are:

- Unresolved resentments and anger
- Loneliness

- Boredom
- Fear
- Anxiety
- Frustration
- Low self-esteem
- Shame (feeling useless, worthless, and/or unlovable)
- Stress
- Feeling unappreciated
- Sadness or grief
- An unmet need for validation and/or affection
- A few of the more common *external triggers* for sexual acting out are:
- Unstructured time alone
- Travel (especially when traveling alone)
- Relationship strain and/or breakups
- Unexpected life changes (job, finances, tragedies, etc.)
- Highly stimulating positive experiences (like buying a home or getting a new job)
- Drug and/or alcohol use/abuse
- Unexpected exposure to sexual stimuli (a lingerie catalog, a sexy billboard, encountering an attractive person, etc.)
- Arguments (especially with loved ones and authority figures)
- Reprimands
- Financial insecurity
- Trouble within the family (like a child struggling at school)
- An emotionally or physically unavailable spouse

The following exercise is designed to help you identify your primary triggers toward addiction.

List internal triggers for your sexual behavior. After you complete your list, place an asterisk (*) next to the triggers that you struggle with the most.

Example: *Feeling depressed and alone.*

_____

_____

_____

_____

_____

List external triggers for your sexual behavior. After you complete your list, place an asterisk (*) next to the ones that you struggle with the most.

Example: *Driving past a strip club.*

_____

_____

_____

_____

_____

Based on the previous two questions, create a list of your top five most powerful triggers.

_____

_____

_____

_____

_____

For each of your top five triggers, list a healthy activity you can turn to instead of your addiction.

Example: *I am triggered when I feel lonely. Instead of acting out, I can call my 12-step sexual recovery sponsor and tell him/her how I'm feeling.*

_____

_____

_____

_____

_____

_____

_____

_____

_____

_____

Exercise 9: The Cycle of Sexual Addiction

Sexual addiction is cyclical in nature, with no clear beginning or end and one stage of the cycle leading to the next (and then the next). Today, most sex addiction treatment specialists divide the cycle of sexual addiction into six distinct stages.

- **Stage One—Triggers:** As discussed in Exercise 8, triggers are catalysts that create a need/desire to act out sexually. Triggers can be internal or external in nature. If triggers are not dealt with in a healthy way (dissipated via a healthy, non-addictive coping mechanism like talking to supportive friends, family members, or a therapist), then the cycle inevitably slides forward into stage two.
- **Stage Two—Fantasy:** After being triggered, you automatically turn to your primary coping mechanism (sexual fantasy). In short, you start thinking about how much you enjoyed past sexual encounters and how much you would enjoy a sexual encounter either right now or in the near future. These fantasies do not involve memories of bad experiences or unwanted consequences. Once you are mired in fantasy, it is very difficult to stop the addictive cycle.
- **Stage Three—Ritualization:** Ritualization is where fantasy moves toward reality. For example, you log on to the computer and go to your favorite porn site, or you hop in the car and drive to a place where sex workers congregate, or you begin the process of booking an out-of-town business trip on which you can act out sexually without restraint, or whatever. This stage of the cycle is also known as *the bubble* or *the trance* because you *lose touch with reality* in it. This stage of the addiction, rather than actually having sex, provides the escapist neurochemical high that you seek.
- **Stage Four—Acting Out:** Most non-sex addicts think that this stage, rather than stage three, is the ultimate goal of sexual addiction, because this is where actual sex and orgasm takes place (either solo or with another person or people). However, as stated above, the fantasy-fueled escape and dissociation of stage three is your real objective. In fact, if you're like most sex addicts, you try to postpone this stage for as long as you can because *orgasm ends your escapist high.*
- **Stage Five—Distancing/Numbing:** After you act out sexually, you try to distance yourself emotionally from what you've just done. Basically, your thinking is now focused on "damage control," and you engage in various forms of denial—blaming,

justifying, rationalizing, etc. You do this in an attempt to protect yourself from stage six of the cycle.

- **Stage Six—Despair (Shame/Anxiety/Depression):** Over time, distancing/numbing fades and becomes less effective. And when it does, you start to feel shame and remorse about your secret sexual life. Exacerbating these unwanted emotions is the fact that you feel powerless over your addiction. Plus, whatever reality you were trying to escape in the first place returns, bringing with it the same emotional discomfort you were feeling before. And, as you may recall, emotional discomfort is exactly what triggered your addiction in the first place. In other words, stage six spins the self-perpetuating cycle right back to stage one.

The following exercise is designed to help you understand your addictive cycle by examining the events and feelings that occur before, during, and after you sexually act out. The ultimate goal in understanding your cycle is finding ways to stop the cycle before you engage in an addictive behavior.

List your top five triggers toward sexual acting out (from Exercise 8). For any external triggers, attach one or more feelings to that trigger.

Example: *Driving past a strip club. I feel curious, excited, and agitated.*

_____

_____

_____

_____

_____

Briefly describe, in non-graphic terms, five sexual fantasies that you commonly engage in after you are triggered toward sexual addiction.

Example: *I think about having sex with my assistant or some other younger female, and how hot that will be.*

_____

_____

_____

_____

_____

_____

_____

_____

_____

_____

Briefly describe, in non-graphic terms, five rituals that precede your addictive sexual behaviors. Rituals are often (but not always) related to the fantasies described above. Note how long you typically intend to engage in this activity, and how long you typically do engage in this activity.

Example: *I go online and look at porn, thinking I will only do so for a few minutes, but then I end up doing it for several hours, constantly searching for a better, hotter video.*

_____

_____

_____

_____

_____

_____

_____

_____

_____

List, in non-graphic, non-sexualized language, five ways in which you sexually act out. Sexual acting out is usually (but not always) a direct extension (logical conclusion) of the rituals described above.

Example: *I hire a prostitute, paying for oral sex.*

_____

_____

_____

_____

_____

List five ways in which you distance yourself from your behavior after you act out—blaming, justifying, minimizing, rationalizing, etc.

Example: *I tell myself that this time wasn't as bad as the time before.*

_____

_____

_____

_____

_____

List five examples of the despair that eventually kicks in after you've acted out.

Example: *I feel as if I will never be able to stop these horrible behaviors.*

_____

_____

_____

_____

_____

What have you learned about your sex addiction cycle? How do you feel after completing this exercise?

_____

_____

_____

_____

_____

Section Three: Relapse Prevention

An ounce of prevention is worth a pound of cure.
—Benjamin Franklin

Exercise 10: Basic Tools for Sexual Sobriety

Unfortunately, triggers for sexual addiction are unavoidable. There will always be an attractive person walking by, a billboard that gets your attention, or an unexpectedly sexy scene in a movie. Such is life. You will encounter triggers on a regular basis no matter what you do. Recognizing this, it is helpful to have a set of easily utilized in-the-moment tools you can turn to when triggered (or think that you might be triggered). A few tools you may wish to develop and implement include:

- **Bookending:** You can arrange to "bookend" potentially triggering events with phone calls to a supportive friend in recovery. During the "before" call you commit to sobriety, and you may even discuss plans to avoid relapse. The "after" call provides an opportunity to discuss what happened, what feelings came up, and what you might need to do differently next time.
- **Gratitude:** A great way to combat "stinking thinking" is to create a gratitude list. Writing a ten-item gratitude list nearly always counteracts almost any trigger and halts the addictive cycle.
- **HALT (an acronym for Hungry, Angry/Anxious, Lonely, and Tired):** As a sex addict, you must learn to ask yourself: When is the last time I ate? Did I get enough sleep last night? Is there some conflict in my life that I need to resolve? Would a few minutes spent talking with someone who understands me help me to feel better? More often than not, a catnap, a candy bar, or a five minute phone conversation will greatly diminish your desire to sexually act out.
- **Rubber Banding:** With this, you place a rubber band around your wrist, and whenever you recognize an addictive sexual thought or fantasy you pull the rubber band and release it so it snaps against your arm—ouch!—as a way to distract yourself.
- **The Three-Second Rule:** As a sex addict, you cannot control the thoughts you have or the fact that you feel triggered. You can, however, control what you do with those thoughts and feelings. For instance, after spotting an attractive person, you can acknowledge that you are human and it is normal to feel an attraction. However, as a sex addict, you need to turn away from the triggering individual *within three seconds*. Then, without turning back for another look, you should think about the other person as someone's wife/daughter/sister or father/son/brother, wishing that individual and

his or her family all the best. In short, when you catch yourself objectifying another person, you immediately turn away and try to humanize that person.

- **Turning It Over:** This is a variation of the three-second rule described above. Essentially, after recognizing an addictive sexual thought or fantasy, you give yourself a maximum of three seconds to turn away from it and focus on something else—the score of last night's game, what you need from the grocery store, how much you love your spouse, the trouble your kid is having with algebra, etc. Of course, during difficult periods unwanted sexual thoughts may pop into your head almost constantly; one unwanted fantasy is banished and moments later another arrives. When this occurs, the three-second rule and turning it over can be used repeatedly.

Of course, the half-dozen tools listed above are hardly the full arsenal. Other in-the-moment sobriety tools that you may want to think about include:

- Journaling
- Attending an online support group or meeting
- Prayer and/or meditation
- Reading recovery related literature
- Written 12-step work
- 12-step sponsorship (and similar forms of ongoing outreach to other recovering sex addicts)
- Any activity listed in the outer boundary of your sexual sobriety plan

Create a list of in-the-moment sobriety tools that you think will work for you. Write a sentence about why you believe each of these tools will be effective. Describe a way to create something physical (or digital) that will help you to implement each of these tools.

Example: *Bookending. I have lots of work-related social events, and I know that I may be triggered at them. If I commit to sobriety before each event and check in afterward, I will have an extra layer of protection against my addiction. I can add numbers of friends in recovery to my phone, making it easy to call someone and bookend a potentially problematic event.*

Tool 1: _____

_____

_____

_____

Tool 2: _____

_____

_____

_____

Tool 3: _____

_____

_____

_____

Tool 4: _____

_____

_____

_____

Tool 5: _____

_____

_____

_____

Exercise 11: Recognizing and Managing Stress

Stress is a primary trigger toward relapse for most recovering sex addicts. As such, it is important to understand the various areas of your life that cause you to feel stress, and to develop at least a few effective stress management techniques. For most of us, stress centers around work, school, finances, romance, sex, and/or family. Other potential stressors include self-care (food, exercise, sleep, etc.), physical health (illness, injury, aging, etc.), losses (death, moving, job change, etc.), social life, hobbies, and religion/spirituality.

There are countless ways to manage stress. For ideas, take a look at the outer boundary of your sexual sobriety plan. Beyond what you have listed in your outer boundary, you might consider the following:

- Journaling
- Meditating
- Doing fun things (games, outings, movies, and the like) with your spouse, kids, friends, etc.
- Exercising, especially on a team or with others
- Developing a new hobby or enjoying an old one
- Being emotionally intimate with your spouse
- Reading recovery oriented literature
- Going to 12-step meetings, therapy, and/or faith-based support groups
- Taking a class for fun or to further your professional life
- Gardening
- Sprucing up the house
- Caring for a pet
- Taking a warm, relaxing bath
- Music—playing it or listening to it
- Going for a hike or walk or otherwise spending time in nature

List areas of your life that cause you stress, either regularly or sporadically. Note the frequency with which stress arises in each area, and the severity of that stress.

Example: *Finances. I worry about money constantly. The stress is ongoing. Depending on my bank account, my anxiety ranges from moderate to severe.*

_____

_____

_____

_____

_____

_____

_____

_____

_____

_____

Based on the above list, pick your three most common/severe areas for stress, and list the specific ways in which that stress manifests.

Example: *Money: I feel anxious when we're planning for vacations, and I can't relax when we're on those vacations because I'm worried that we can't afford whatever it is we're doing. I get irritable and tense when I should be enjoying myself. I get short-tempered with my family because they're having fun while I'm feeling stressed out.*

Stressor Number One: _____

_____

_____

Stressor Number Two: _____

_____

_____

Stressor Number Three: _____

_____

_____

What, if any, are your most effective stress management techniques?

Example: *When I feel stressed, I take three deep breaths, and then I tell myself that everything will be OK.*

_____

_____

_____

_____

_____

List activities you are willing to commit to on a regular basis in order to become a more calm and centered person. These should be action items, preferably engaged in with other people.

Example: *I am committed to attending a weekly meditation and yoga class.*

_____

_____

_____

_____

_____

Exercise 12: Creating Your Serenity Spot

In Exercise 11, meditation was suggested as a potential stress management technique. However, most recovering sex addicts, especially those new to the process, find it incredibly difficult to "sit quietly and empty their minds." In fact, when they try to meditate in this way they typically find themselves either obsessing about the past or future tripping (worrying about things that *might* happen in the future). If that is the case for you, developing a peaceful and safe serenity spot that you can visit when meditating may be extremely helpful.

> NOTE: This is a visualization exercise. You may want to record the instructions below on your smartphone or some other digital device, and then you can listen to the instructions as you close your eyes and visualize.

Instructions for creating your serenity spot are as follows:

- Find a quiet, comfortable space.
- Turn off your TV, radio, phone, and anything else that makes noise or that might interrupt you.
- When you are ready, sit with both of your feet on the floor and your hands placed lightly above your knees.
- Close your eyes and take some deep, slow, relaxing breaths.
- As you relax and breathe, let your mind wander with the idea of finding your serenity spot.
- Your serenity spot should be secluded, meaning you are protected from intruders, attacks, and interruptions.
- Your serenity spot can be a place you have been to. It can also be a place you have seen on TV or in a movie, or that you've read about in a book. Or it can be totally imaginary, original to you and you alone. It can be in nature, your home, or any other relaxing environment.
- Give yourself as much time as you need, allowing your serenity spot to materialize instead of forcing it to appear. There is no rush. If you can't find your serenity spot today, that's OK. You can try this exercise again tomorrow.
- Once you locate your serenity spot, notice everything that you see in all directions. Turn around and take a 360 degree look.

- Is it day or night in your space? What is the quality of the light? What colors do you see? Can you see the sun (or the moon, if it's nighttime)?
- Now feel the ground beneath your feet. What is it like? Is it dry, moist, grainy, fine, smooth, rough, or something else? Is it soft? Can you run it through your fingers?
- What do you hear? Are there birds and animals? Is there water nearby—perhaps a stream or even the ocean? Is the wind rustling through the trees?
- What does the air feel like? Is it dry, moist, or something in between? Is it warm or cool? Does it feel heavy on your skin, or light?
- What can you smell? Are there flowers nearby? If so, what kind? Can you smell trees and grass, the mossy earth, or the ocean? Can you taste any of the odors?
- Now let yourself relax and enjoy your serenity spot for as long as you wish.
- Eventually, when you feel ready, let yourself return from your serenity spot, knowing you can visit it again any time you'd like, for as long as you'd like.

After you have returned from your serenity spot, describe it below as thoroughly as you can. Be sure to cover all of your five senses—sight, sound, smell, taste, and touch. Try to also describe the sensation of comfort and safety that your serenity spot gives you.

_____

_____

_____

_____

_____

_____

_____

_____

_____

_____

_____

_____

Exercise 13: Your Personal Sobriety Reminder

Imagine that a dear friend or loved one has written a letter for you to read just before you start to act out. What could that person say to you to keep you from it? Perhaps the letter would read as follows:

Dear XXXXX:

If you're reading this note, it's probably because you are feeling triggered and you're thinking about violating your sexual boundary plan. Maybe you just saw some incredibly hot person and now you're thinking about sex. More likely, however, you are feeling lonely, anxious, depressed, ashamed, or bored, and you don't want to feel this way. So you're thinking about the excitement of illicit sex because you know that will take you away from your emotional discomfort.

It is possible that you're thinking about calling an old sex partner, looking at porn, checking out a hookup app, or hiring a prostitute. Any and all of these actions would violate your sexual boundary plan. You may be thinking about these things even though you know that once you get started with addictive sexual behaviors, you can't seem to stop.

If you give in to these urges, you'll find yourself right back in the cycle of sexual addiction, and your life will start to fall apart just like it did before. You'll waste incredible amounts of time and money. You'll lose focus. You'll put yourself at risk for STDs. You'll feel ashamed about your behavior and your inability to keep the commitments you've made to yourself and your family. You'll start lying and keeping secrets as a way to cover up your bad behavior. You'll ruin your marriage. You'll put your career and your standing in the community at risk. You might even get arrested. Worst of all, you will feel incredibly depressed and anxious—maybe even suicidal.

I know you don't want those things. You've been there before and it was awful. So instead of acting out and ruining your sobriety, call your wife just to hear her voice. Play a game with your kids. Walk the dog. Get started on that big project at work. Read a book. Call a friend in recovery. Paint the house. Take a nap. Plan a family vacation. Eat a candy bar. Go to the gym. Volunteer at the local soup kitchen. Do whatever it is that you have to do to break the cycle of your addiction, and do it right now. Because the sooner you stop the cycle, the better off you will be.

When you are not acting out sexually, your life is better. You know this. And the longer you are sexually sober, the better it gets. You feel more connected to other people, you are more focused at work, and you are more present with your family. Your finances are better. You enjoy the company of other people, and they enjoy you in return. You no longer need to compartmentalize, hide, and lie about huge chunks of your life. You are happy.

If you are still unsure what to do right now, ask yourself: If my wife and kids could see what I was thinking about doing, how would I feel about that? If you would feel good, then proceed. Otherwise, think about doing something else. And no matter what, remember that even though you may be feeling worthless and unlovable right now, you're not. You are lovable and worthwhile, and you deserve a happy, healthy, emotionally fulfilling life. Sex addiction will not bring you that. Sexual sobriety will.

Sincerely,
XXXXX

Would you like to have a sobriety reminder like the one above that you could turn to in times of need? If so, you can. In fact, you're going to write that reminder now.

Address your reminder letter to you, from you, and be sure to include the following:

- **What might be happening that would cause you to reach for this letter**
- **What you might be thinking about doing that would violate your sexual boundary plan**
- **What will happen if you act out in this (or some other) way**
- **What you can do that will stop the cycle of your sexual addiction**
- **What your life can/will look like if you don't act out**

_____

_____

_____

_____

_____

_____

_____

_____

_____

_____

_____

_____

_____

_____

_____

_____

_____

_____

_____

_____

_____

_____

_____

_____

_____

_____

_____

_____

_____

_____

_____

Exercise 14: Your Emergency Exit Plan

As a recovering sex addict, you will be triggered to act out sexually. It's going to happen, and that's a fact, and there is nothing you can do to stop it. Recognizing this, it is helpful to have an emergency exit plan in place, and to practice the concrete steps of this plan until your ability to step away from the cycle of your addiction becomes ingrained and automatic.

As with any emergency exit plan, from tornado drills in grammar school to earthquake drills in your office high-rise, there are three essential elements:

- An obvious and unmistakable alarm signal
- A straightforward plan for escape
- A way to practice this plan so that, when needed, you can exit automatically

If you're like most recovering sex addicts you have both obvious and discreet alarms. Obvious alarms would be engaging in any middle boundary activity—arguing with your partner, skipping therapy or a 12-step meeting, driving through an iffy neighborhood for no reason, etc. Less obvious alarms tend to involve emotional discomfort—depression, anxiety, shame, boredom, anger, loneliness, etc. In short, pretty much anything in your middle boundary or your list of triggers qualifies as an alarm.

The steps you can take in response to an alarm also tend to be straightforward. You can call your sponsor or a friend in recovery, go to a meeting, pray, meditate, exercise, spend time with your kids, etc. In fact, anything in your outer circle will likely work.

As for a routine way to learn these steps? You do this the same way you learned about fire and earthquake safety—practice, practice, practice. And you don't need to be in crisis to practice. For instance, if one of your healthy responses to an alarm signal is calling a friend in recovery, you can practice *when you're feeling good* by calling to check in and to ask how that person is doing. You might even suggest that the two of you do something fun and social—see a movie, go bowling, have lunch, etc. Over time, using the phone when you don't need help makes it a lot easier to use the phone when you actually do need assistance.

Create your personalized emergency exit plan below, with ten alarms, ten healthy responses, and ten practice techniques. Be as specific as possible. When your emergency exit plan is completed, practice your healthy responses, one (or more) per day until you have been through your list at least three times.

Example:

Alarm Signal—Feeling anxiety and wanting to escape that feeling with pornography

> *Healthy Response—Call my sponsor or a friend in recovery to talk about what I am feeling*

> *Practice Technique—Call that person just to say hi and to see how they are doing*

Alarm Signal 1: _____

    Healthy Response: _____

    Practice Technique: _____

Alarm Signal 2: _____

    Healthy Response: _____

    Practice Technique: _____

Alarm Signal 3: _____

    Healthy Response: _____

    Practice Technique: _____

Alarm Signal 4: _____

    Healthy Response: _____

    Practice Technique: _____

Alarm Signal 5: _____

    Healthy Response: _____

    Practice Technique: _____

Alarm Signal 6: _____

    Healthy Response: _____

    Practice Technique: _____

Alarm Signal 7: _____

    Healthy Response: _____

    Practice Technique:_____

Alarm Signal 8: _____

    Healthy Response: _____

    Practice Technique: _____

Alarm Signal 9: _____

    Healthy Response: _____

    Practice Technique: _____

Alarm Signal 10: _____

    Healthy Response: _____

    Practice Technique: _____

Exercise 15: Creating Your Portable Toolkit

The time has come for you to create an actual toolkit, packed with tools for sexual sobriety, that you can carry around with you at all times, opening it up when you are triggered and grabbing whatever tool is needed. Consider purchasing a briefcase, messenger bag, portfolio, or some other bag to house your tools. Do not jumble your tools into a case that you also use for work or some other purpose. Your sexual sobriety toolkit needs to be discrete and easily assessable, and you should not have to search through other stuff to locate the tools within it.

Items you might want in your toolkit include:

- A printed version of your sexual boundary plan (Exercise 4)
- A printed list of helpful phone numbers—therapist, 12-step sponsor, friends in recovery, etc.
- 12-step meeting lists (and meeting lists for any other support groups you attend)
- Photos of your spouse and kids
- Rubber bands
- Candy bars (or a healthier snack)
- A list of things for which you are grateful
- A list of effective stress management techniques (Exercise 11)
- Meditation aids, including a description of your serenity spot (Exercise 12)
- Your written reminder about the importance of sobriety (Exercise 13)
- Your emergency exit plan (Exercise 14)
- Recovery related literature
- Your recovery journal
- Etc.

Many sex addicts also like to keep digitized versions of these items (if they can be digitized, and almost all of them can) on their smartphones, tablets, laptops, and other digital devices.

List the items that you want in your portable toolkit, with a brief statement about when and how each particular item might help you.

_____

_____

_____

_____

_____

_____

_____

_____

_____

_____

_____

_____

_____

Now create your portable toolkit. After you have done so, write a few sentences about how your portable toolkit makes you feel (safe, protected, prepared, etc.)

_____

_____

_____

_____

_____

Section Four: Working On Your Underlying Issues

We fear violence less than our own feelings. Personal, private, solitary pain is more terrifying than what anyone else can inflict.
—Jim Morrison

Exercise 16: Understanding Your History

For the most part, sex addicts engage in compulsive sexual behaviors as a way to self-medicate emotional discomfort. Much of the time this emotional discomfort is more about their life history than current events. Knowing this, it is important for you to fully examine your life, in particular your sexual history, your substance use history, your relationship/intimacy history, your school/work history, and other critical life events. Doing this lends perspective to your addiction, revealing connections between the past and the present, helping you understand more about when, where, why, and how your addiction started. At the same time, this exercise helps you understand the impact of your sexually compulsive behaviors.

> NOTE: To complete this exercise, you will need a roll of butcher paper or several individual sheets of paper taped together, plus five different colored pens or fine-point markers.

To begin, you need to identify key early-life events (age 0 to 10) in your sexual history—strong memories, traumatic events, events that evoke strong feelings, sexual abuse, etc. First list your age, then list the event.

Example: *Age 7, I walked in on my older sister when she was masturbating.*

_____

_____

_____

_____

_____

Now, using the same age/incident format, identify key adolescent events (age 10 to 18) in your sexual history—strong memories, traumatic events, events that evoke strong feelings, sexual abuse, etc.

Example: *Age 13, I looked at porn on the Internet for the first time.*

_____

_____

_____

_____

_____

Now, using the same age/incident format, identify key young adult events (age 18 to 25) in your sexual history—strong memories, traumatic events, events that evoke strong feelings, sexual abuse, etc.

Example: *Age 19, I got pregnant during my freshman year of college and had an abortion.*

_____

_____

_____

_____

_____

Now, using the same age/incident format, identify key adult events (age 25 and up) in your sexual history—strong memories, traumatic events, events that evoke strong feelings, sexual abuse, etc.

Example: *Age 32, I was physically assaulted and robbed by a man I met online and invited over for sex.*

_____

_____

_____

_____

_____

Now, using the same age/incident format, identify key events in your substance use/abuse history—first use, escalation, consequences, events that evoke strong feelings, etc.

Example: *Age 16, I drank so much that I had to go to the emergency room for alcohol poisoning.*

_____

_____

_____

_____

_____

Now, using the same age/incident format, identify key events in your relationship history—first dates, important relationships, breakups, marriages, divorces, etc.

Example: *Age 20, Marie and I got married (mostly because she was pregnant).*

_____

_____

_____

_____

_____

Now, using the same age/incident format, identify key events in your school/work history—successes, failures, awards, reprimands, etc.

Example: *Age 18, I graduated from high school with honors.*

_____

_____

_____

_____

_____

Now, using the same age/incident format, identify key critical life events (unrelated to sex, substance use/abuse, romance, or work/school)—births, deaths, military service, moving across the country, fights with important friends, etc.

Example: *Age 29, my grandmother, who'd always been my go-to person for advice, passed away.*

_____

_____

_____

_____

_____

Using your roll of butcher paper or your taped-together sheets of paper, draw a long horizontal line from one end to the other. (Most sex addicts find they need a line that is at least five or six feet long.) Now divide the line into decades—0 to 10, 10 to 20, etc., up to your current age. Using a red pen, add all of your key sexual events to the timeline, writing your age above the line and a brief notation of the event below the line. Using a blue pen, add all of your key substance use/abuse events to the timeline. Next, do the same with your key relationship events (purple pen), school/work events (black pen), and other critical life events (green pen).

Example:

... 13 (red)	16 (blue)	18 (black)	19 (red)	20 (purple)	29 (green) ...
First Porn	ER for Booze	HS Grad	First Prostitute	Got Married	Grandma Died

Briefly describe any patterns that you now see in your life, in particular the ways in which your addiction relates to other life events and experiences.

_____

_____

_____

_____

_____

Looking at your timeline, what have been the ten worst moments in your life, sexual or otherwise?

_____

_____

_____

_____

_____

_____

_____

_____

_____

_____

Of your ten worst moments, pick one that seems significant and describe the ways in which you think it has impacted your sexual addiction.

_____

_____

_____

_____

_____

Exercise 17: Nature vs. Nurture

Sex addicts often want to know why they are sexually addicted. Sometimes they struggle to move forward with recovery until they have an answer. If that is the case for you, this exercise can help.

Generally speaking, there are two main causes of addiction (all types): nature (genetics) and nurture (environment). Genetic influences are most easily evidenced by a family history of addiction and/or mental illness. Environmental factors typically center on unresolved trauma, early exposure to an addictive substance or behavior, and social stimuli. Most sex addicts report a combination of genetic and environmental influences. This exercise looks at both issues.

List any family members who've struggled with a mental illness, noting whether they've been formally diagnosed and treated.

Example: *My mother suffers from depression and periods of manic behavior. She has consistently refused to see any kind of psychiatrist or mental health counselor, so she is undiagnosed and untreated.*

_____

_____

_____

_____

_____

List any family members who've struggled with addiction, noting whether they've been formally diagnosed and if they're in recovery.

Example: *My father is an alcoholic. He has been going to AA since I was 17.*

_____

_____

_____

_____

_____

List traumatic events that may have affected your sexual outlook. (Trauma will be covered more thoroughly in Exercise 18. For now, just do your best.)

Example: *I found my dad's stash of BDSM magazines and videos when I was ten, and it really freaked me out.*

_____

_____

_____

_____

_____

_____

_____

_____

_____

How do you feel about your family history and your trauma history? Do you feel that your addiction is the fault of others, or do you think that you are responsible for the choices you've made?

_____

_____

_____

_____

_____

If none of the information above feels like it relates to your sexual addiction, how and why do you think you became sexually addicted?

_____

_____

_____

_____

_____

Exercise 18: Trauma (Understanding Victimization and Abuse)

Generally speaking, trauma (victimization and abuse) is defined as any event or experience (including witnessing) that is physically and/or psychologically overwhelming in the moment and/or later, when the event is remembered. Trauma is highly subjective, meaning incidents that are highly traumatic to one person might not be traumatic for another. For instance, a fender-bender might be much more distressing for a new mother with her baby in the car than for a professional racecar driver.

Early-life trauma typically occurs in one or more of the following forms:

- **Threatening Behavior:** any action or spoken threat to hurt another person physically, psychologically, emotionally, or sexually
- **Psychological Abuse:** emotional abuse (mind games) intended to cause fear and/or confusion in the victim
- **Physical Abuse:** any forceful or violent physical action designed to intimidate or to make another person do something against his or her will
- **Sexual Abuse:** any non-consenting sexual act or behavior, including behaviors "consented to" by minors, adults who are inebriated, and mentally handicapped people

People who were traumatized (victimized and abused) as children are at high risk for addiction and other psychological disorders. In fact, research shows that survivors of multiple instances of childhood trauma are seven times more likely to become alcoholic and eleven times more likely to use intravenous drugs. They are also much more likely to become sexually addicted. In particular, childhood sexual abuse (both overt and covert) is linked to sexual addiction. That said, sex abuse is by no means a prerequisite for sexual addiction.

Sadly, victims of abuse (of any type) tend to perpetuate the behavior, becoming abusers themselves. In other words, being abused and becoming an abuser seem to go hand in hand.

As a recovering sex addict, it can be very helpful to unravel strands of your trauma history, looking at the ways in which you were victimized and abused, and also the ways in which you have victimized and abused others. In doing so, you will hopefully gain a better understanding of how you developed certain behavior patterns and locked into your addictive cycle.

NOTE: Formalized treatment of trauma is a difficult and unpleasant process. Nevertheless, many recovering sex addicts find this work worthwhile, as it addresses a major underlying issue driving their addictive behaviors. That said, *extensive trauma work should not be attempted until sexual sobriety is firmly established.* Otherwise, the emotional pain of trauma therapy could easily trigger a relapse.

List important instances in your life in which you may have been abused/victimized. Briefly note your age, the category of abuse, the perpetrator, and how it occurred.

Example: *Age 11 to 15. Physical abuse. My older brother. He would hit me when nobody else was around.*

_____

_____

_____

_____

_____

_____

_____

_____

_____

_____

List important instances in your life in which you feel that you may have victimized others. Briefly note the category of abuse, your victim, and what you did.

Example: *Psychological abuse. My wife. After I cheated, I blamed it on her, calling her frigid and ugly.*

_____

_____

_____

_____

_____

_____

_____

_____

_____

_____

Do you see any connections between your history of being traumatized and your history of hurting others? If so, describe those links?

_____

_____

_____

_____

Have you previously addressed trauma issues in your life? If so, in what ways, with whom, and do you feel this work was successful? If not, do you think that once you've established a modicum of sexual sobriety you will want to embark on this emotionally painful process? If so, why? If not, why not?

_____

_____

_____

_____

Exercise 19: Guilt, Shame, and Your Distorted Sense of Self

Guilt and shame are not the same thing. Guilt is a healthy and necessary sense that you have violated your moral code, values, and standards, or that you have stepped on someone else's rights. Shame is a sense of being a failure as a person, of not being good enough, of feeling doubt about yourself at your very core. If you feel shame, you feel as if there is something fundamentally wrong with you as a person.

Examples of Guilt:

- I made a mistake.
- I did a bad thing.
- My behavior was hurtful.

Examples of Shame:

- I am a mistake.
- I am a bad person.
- I am defective and unlovable.

Guilt is a healthy human emotion that tells us we have done something wrong and we need to correct or amend our behavior. Shame, on the other hand, is an internal feeling of "badness" that consistently flares up, especially if/when we are acting out sexually. Guilt implies: "I did something regrettable and I feel badly (i.e., guilty) about my actions." Shame implies: "I did something regrettable because I am a bad person, and there is nothing at all that I can do about that." Guilt is a positive force in terms of changing behavior, while shame is quite the opposite.

Shame also leads to a distorted self-image—negative beliefs that inaccurately color the way we see ourselves and the world. For sex addicts, a distorted (mostly negative) self-image can be highly destructive. Consider the following belief, held by many sex addicts: *I am a bad person, unworthy of love and true connection.* A distorted view of self like that can and often does lead to the following thoughts, feelings, and behaviors:

- I can't tell anyone about my acting out, or they'll know how awful I am.
- I will pretend to be "normal," smiling and acting as if everything is OK no matter how miserable and depressed I get.

- I will "get mine" as revenge for being shorted in life, acting out whenever and wherever I feel like it without regard for others.

Sadly, sex addicts often feel shame more than guilt, with shame creating a distorted and mostly negative self-image. In other words, sex addicts often feel as if something within themselves is the cause and crux of their problem, as if they are flawed in some deeply meaningful way and therefore doomed to a life of misery, isolation, and regrettable behaviors. Often, they need a great deal of time before they even begin to understand that they are not inherently defective, that it was their maladaptive choices and not their true selves that caused their addiction and its related negative consequences.

The good news is that once you finally begin to understand that you are a good person who has behaved badly rather than a bad person who was just doing what bad people do, your process of healing can truly begin.

The most effective way to combat shame and a distorted self-image is by stating affirmations to the contrary. Affirmations are powerful messages that confirm your worth, reminding you that who you are today is okay and enough. Affirmations validate that you are not defined by past behaviors, no matter how bad they were. Affirmations are stated aloud daily, often several times per day, as a way to replace your shame-distorted sense of self with self-esteem.

Many recovering sex addicts, especially those new to the healing process, struggle to come up with positive affirmations. If that is the case for you, the following list may help:

- I am working my recovery.
- I am an imperfect yet worthwhile person.
- I have value and worth.
- I can love myself and accept my past.
- I am a worthwhile person, exactly as God intended me to be.
- I am finding my integrity one day at a time.
- I am worthy of love and acceptance, exactly as I am.
- Today, I choose to live in the moment.
- My past actions do not define me in the present.
- I am able to give and receive love.
- I respect the boundaries of others.
- I am recovering with the help of others.
- I have done bad things, but I am not a bad person.
- It is OK for me to talk to others about what I am thinking and feeling.

- I let go of my shame.
- I am fully present today.
- I can heal and forgive myself for the harms I have caused.
- I am a better person today than I was yesterday.
- I am able to ask for and accept help when I need it, without feeling ashamed.
- Today, I choose to reach out to others before I act out.

List the things that you feel the most shame about. In all likelihood, these are secrets that you were planning to take to the grave.

Example: *I gave my wife an STD, and then I accused her of cheating on me.*

_____

_____

_____

_____

_____

_____

_____

_____

_____

Pick the five most shameful (emotionally painful) items from list above. For each of these, describe how shame has distorted your self-image, and then list three contrary affirmations.

Example:
Shame—I gave my wife an STD, and then I accused her of cheating on me.
Distorted Self-Image—I am a bad person, and I don't deserve to be loved.
Contrary Affirmations—I am not defined by the mistakes I have made; I can love myself and accept my past; I am recovering with the help and love of others.

Shame: _____

Distorted Self-Image: _____

Contrary Affirmations: _____

_____

_____

Shame: _____

Distorted Self-Image: _____

Contrary Affirmations: _____

_____

_____

Shame: _____

Distorted Self-Image: _____

Contrary Affirmations: _____

_____

_____

Shame: _____

Distorted Self-Image: _____

Contrary Affirmations: _____

_____

_____

Shame: _____

Distorted Self-Image: _____

Contrary Affirmations: _____

_____

_____

Exercise 20: Understanding Your Dependency Needs

As infants, all human beings have the three primary needs—food and water (sustenance), shelter, and emotional connection (love and stimulation). Infants are dependent on others for all three needs. Without the first two, they will die. Without the third, they become depressed and they fail to develop and thrive.

These three basic needs do not go away as we grow older. We still need sustenance, shelter, and emotional connection as adults. And the consequences of going without are exactly the same, including depression and a failure to thrive when our basic need for emotional support is not met. Admittedly, this need looks different and is met in different ways during our adult years, but it does not disappear.

Examples of healthy adult emotional dependency needs are as follows:

- When I'm angry and I tell someone how angry I am, I want/need them to validate what I am feeling (to support, agree with, or at least acknowledge my anger).
- When I'm sad and I express my sadness to others, I want/need them to support, empathize with, and soothe me.
- When I'm joyous and I express this to others, I want/need them to validate, mirror, and cheer for me.

The simple truth is that emotionally healthy people naturally reach out to others—spouses, family members, longtime friends, lovers, therapists, clergy, support groups, and the like—when they have strong emotions, good or bad, that they need to regulate and process. But addicts, usually because they were not properly nurtured as infants (and therefore learned that others could not be trusted to meet their emotional dependency needs), find it very difficult to reach out to others for support. Instead, they turn to alcohol, drugs, sex, food, or some other addictive substance or behavior, using that as a way to temporarily numb out and not feel their emotions.

Below is a list of emotional dependency needs created by the Center for Nonviolent Communication. The list is neither exhaustive nor definitive. It is simply a starting point from which you can begin the process of identifying the unmet needs that drive your behavior. As you examine this list, think hard about which items do and do not seem important to you, remembering that every person is unique, so every person has his or her own set of dependency needs. In other words, there are no right or wrong dependency needs.

NOTE: This exercise may create feelings of frustration and disappointment because you've identified needs that are not being met and feel that, because of your sexual addiction, you don't deserve to have them met. For example, you may find it difficult to ask your rightfully angry spouse to be more loving. If so, you may want to initially focus your healing process on people you haven't wounded so deeply, like friends, clergy, siblings, and the like.

EMOTIONAL DEPENDENCY NEEDS

CONNECTION
acceptance
affection
appreciation
belonging
cooperation
communication
closeness
community
companionship
compassion
consideration
consistency
empathy
inclusion
intimacy
love
mutuality
nurturing
respect/self-respect
safety
security
stability
support
to know and be known
to see and be seen
to understand and
 be understood
trust
warmth

HONESTY
authenticity
integrity
presence

PLAY
joy
humor

PEACE
beauty
communion
ease
equality
harmony
inspiration
order

PHYSICAL WELL-BEING
air
food
movement/exercise
rest/sleep
sexual expression
safety
shelter
touch
water

MEANING
awareness
celebration of life
challenge
clarity
competence
consciousness
contribution
creativity
discovery
efficacy
effectiveness
growth
hope
learning
mourning
participation
purpose
self-expression
stimulation
to matter
understanding

AUTONOMY
choice
freedom
independence
space
spontaneity

Pick five significant emotional dependency needs that would help you feel loved and connected. Each person has different needs, so don't worry about picking "the right five." Just pick five that seem important to you. Explain how you would know if each of these needs is being met, and what you might do in the future to get each need met in healthy ways.

Example: *Nurturing. I would know I was being nurtured if I felt like my ideas and beliefs were being thoughtfully considered and given full weight. To feel nurtured, I will need to be more open about what I am thinking and feeling, especially with people I trust (like my spouse). I might even need to tell those people that I'm feeling vulnerable and I really need them to "hear" what I'm saying.*

Need 1: _____

_____

_____

Need 2: _____

_____

_____

Need 3: _____

_____

_____

Need 4: _____

_____

_____

Need 5: _____

_____

_____

List the five most important people in your life and write a sentence about how they do and do not meet your emotional dependency needs. If they are not meeting your needs, do you think they are capable of doing so? If so, how might you facilitate that?

Example: *My husband. I do not feel that my husband meets my need to feel included. I do, however, believe that he does love me, and that he is capable of giving me what I need emotionally. To make this happen, I will need to tell him that I sometimes feel left out. And when I feel left out I will need to remind him of my emotional need, asking him to "bring me in."*

Person 1: _____

_____

_____

Person 2: _____

_____

_____

Person 3: _____

_____

_____

Person 4: _____

_____

_____

Person 5: _____

_____

_____

Section Five: Living (and Enjoying) a Sexually Healthy Life

Life isn't about waiting for the storm to pass. It's about learning to dance in the rain.
—Vivian Greene

Exercise 21: Defining Healthy Sexuality (for You)

Healthy (non-addicted) people innately know that there is more to sex than sex. They know that sex can be as much if not more about emotional intimacy as pure physical pleasure and intensity. Sex addicts, however, have been misusing sexual fantasy and behavior for so long (as a means of self-soothing rather than as a means of connecting) that they can hardly fathom other dimensions of sexuality.

Generally speaking, there are seven dimensions to sex, and, as a recovering sex addict, you'll need to develop your understanding and practice of all seven as part of a healthy, meaningful, and hot sex life. These seven dimensions are as follows:

- Self-nurture—the process of taking care of yourself and feeling better about yourself
- Sensuousness—developing body awareness and learning to stimulate all of the senses
- Relationship intimacy (general)—enjoying the company of others without being sexual
- Partner intimacy—enjoying the company of your significant other without being sexual
- Non-genital sexual touch—giving and feeling physical pleasure without genital contact
- Genital sexuality—enhancing, sustaining, and enriching genital sexuality
- Spiritual intimacy—adding meaning to the above dimensions, and turning sex into an expression of your feelings, values, and sense of connection

List activities, environments, and experiences that you can rely upon for self-nurture, preferably things that involve healthy interactions with other people.

Example: *Taking a boxing class at my gym helps me to feel better physically, to feel better about how I look, and to socialize in a healthy way.*

_____

_____

_____

_____

List activities, environments, and experiences that can help you develop sensuousness (a greater connection to your physical self and the world around you). Think about colors, sounds, smells, textures, tastes, etc.

Example: *Keeping fragrant cut flowers in the house creates pleasure through smell.*

_____

_____

_____

_____

_____

List activities, environments, and experiences that can help you develop general nonsexual relationship intimacy. Think about how you can enjoy the company of others and feel connected to them without being sexual.

Example: *Asking my friends about their lives helps me to know them better and to care more about them.*

_____

_____

_____

_____

_____

List activities, environments, and experiences that can help you develop nonsexual partner intimacy. Think about how you can enjoy the company of your significant other and feel connected to him/her without being sexual.

Example: *Sharing with my spouse about what I am feeling, and not being rejected because of that, helps me to trust and rely upon him/her in new ways.*

_____

_____

_____

_____

_____

List ways you and an intimate partner can experience and enjoy non-genital sexual touch. Think about back rubs, showering together, dressing one another, kissing, and the like.

Example: _When I watch TV with my partner we can hold hands and snuggle._

_____

_____

_____

_____

_____

List ways you and an intimate partner can experience and enjoy emotionally connected genital sexuality. Think about ways you can develop emotional intimacy during sex.

Example: _I can look into my partner's eyes and talk about how much I love him/her while we make love._

_____

_____

_____

_____

_____

List activities, environments, and experiences that can help you develop spiritual intimacy. Think about being honest with your thoughts, feelings, desires, beliefs, moral code, and life priorities.

Example: _I can view my spouse as a child of God with important thoughts and feelings._

_____

_____

_____

_____

_____

Exercise 22: Developing Empathy

As an active sex addict, you almost certainly damaged important relationships, primarily because, while acting out sexually, you didn't think about the ways in which your behaviors were impacting other people. In addition to damaging your romantic relationships, you may have damaged your connections with family members, employers and coworkers, kids, sexual partners, and even yourself. As part of your recovery, it is important that you fully understand the nature and extent of the destruction you have caused, and that you develop empathy (the ability to understand and experience what another person is feeling) for those you have directly and indirectly wounded.

An effective way to do this is to write an empathy letter, which may or may not eventually be read to the person you have harmed. If you have harmed multiple people, you might need to write multiple empathy letters. For instance, if you are single and mostly acted out with anonymous strangers, you can write one letter to yourself and a second letter to the sexual partners you objectified.

DO NOT SHARE YOUR EMPATHY LETTER WITH THE PERSON TO WHOM IT'S ADDRESSED unless you have discussed the letter at length with your therapist, your 12-step sponsor, and others who understand and support your recovery. These are the people who will point out the flaws and weaknesses in your letter, preventing you from sharing it before it is ready and inadvertently causing more harm. Often, your first draft of an empathy letter, no matter how well-intentioned you think you are, will be filled with efforts at manipulation and unwarranted pleas for forgiveness. An empathy letter like that is ineffective at best, counterproductive at worst.

Empathy letters are relatively short (one or two pages at most). In these letters you do the following:

1) Describe exactly what you did (in general, non-graphic terms).
2) Give an apology (without asking the other person to forgive you).
3) Explain that the person you are writing this letter to is in no way at fault, nor did he/she influence your decision to act out at any time.
4) State that you and you alone are responsible for your actions.

5)   Describe the ways in which you have blamed or put down the person you are writing this letter to, perhaps causing that person to doubt his/her perception of reality as a way to hide and/or justify what you were doing.

6)   *Acknowledge the reality of the other person's thoughts and feelings*, which may include hate, disgust, anger, betrayal, rejection, etc. Acknowledge that *you would feel the same way* if the circumstances were reversed.

7)   Accept responsibility for family dysfunction, emotional distancing, and other relationship issues your behavior has created.

8)   Accept responsibility for the emotional, financial, and other burdens and losses your behavior has created.

9)   Describe what you have learned from your behaviors.

10) Describe what your commitments are in terms of changing those behaviors.

Write an empathy letter to your significant other. If you are not in a serious romantic relationship, address your letter to the person (or people) you have hurt the most. (It is possible you will address this letter to yourself.) As mentioned above, if you have harmed multiple people, you may need to write several of these letters.

_____

_____

_____

_____

_____

_____

_____

_____

_____

_____

_____

Exercise 23: For Singles—Your Plan for Healthy Dating

NOTE: If you are already married or in a committed partnership, feel free to skip this exercise, as it is designed for single people who are interested in healthy dating and healthy sexuality. If you are single, you will likely find this exercise highly enlightening and useful.

Most single sex addicts find, after a year or so of solid sexual recovery, that they are ready to think about healthy romance. If this is the case for you, you should develop a workable plan for dating before you begin the process. As with sexual sobriety plans, dating plans can help you understand your goals and what your healthy boundaries are. Once a written plan for healthy dating is in place, you are much less likely to encounter problems (especially problems that might eventually lead to a slip or relapse) in the dating world.

Most recovering sex addicts find the simple "traffic signals dating plan" suggested below to be quite helpful. As you might expect, red lights are characteristics that are unacceptable in anyone you might date. You should agree to not date or to immediately stop dating anyone who displays even one red light trait. Yellow lights are characteristics that should cause you to proceed with caution. Green lights, obviously, are traits that are healthy and desirable in another person.

Each dating plan starts with a list of goals. Write down goals that you have for dating and future relationships.

Example: *I want to be in a monogamous relationship, and to eventually get married.*

_____

_____

_____

_____

_____

List "red light" characteristics that are unacceptable in anyone that you might date. If a person displays even one of these traits, you should immediately stop dating that person.

Example: *I will not date anyone who is already in a long-term romantic relationship.*

_____

_____

_____

_____

_____

List "yellow light" characteristics that would cause you to exercise caution in a particular relationship.

Example: *I will be cautious about a person who is habitually late, especially if that person doesn't call to inform me and apologize.*

_____

_____

_____

_____

_____

List "green light" characteristics that you find desirable in a person you might date.

Example: *I will happily date a person who has lots of different interests, some of which are shared by me.*

_____

_____

_____

_____

_____

Exercise 24: Moving from Shame to Grace

Many recovering sex addicts become so focused on the work of recovery that they forget to have fun. Usually this is because their only real goal early in the process is staying sexually sober. While this is an admirable objective, it doesn't exactly provide them with direction and meaning. Because of this, when the shiny new adventure of recovery inevitably loses its luster, shame creeps back in and they have nowhere to turn for motivation.

If this is the case for you, it may be time to ask yourself: "What are my goals beyond sexual sobriety?" Do you want to start dating? Do you want to join a softball team? Do you want to go on an exciting vacation? Do you want to write a bestselling novel? And if you want those things (or anything else that seems fun but not directly related to recovery), it might be time to expand your outer boundary.

Put another way, there is more to healing from sexual addiction than simply stopping your problem sexual behaviors. You must replace those behaviors with something worthwhile. In the beginning, it may be OK to fill your suddenly available free time with nothing but therapy and meetings, but eventually that gets boring and maybe even depressing. So you must learn to care for yourself in ways that cultivate not only your sobriety but your sense of fun and your enjoyment of life. Interestingly, this process can feel so foreign to some recovering sex addicts that it ends up being the hardest part of the healing process.

A few general esteem building (shame reducing) outer boundary suggestions are as follows:

- Attend to nonsexual friendships
- Spend time in nature
- Do fun things with other people (movies, ballgames, cookouts, and the like)
- Create a "home" at home
- Adopt and care for a pet
- Date
- Find a new hobby
- Exercise
- Develop your spiritual life
- Go on an amazing vacation

- Go to fellowship (coffee or dinner) after 12-step and other support group meetings
- Volunteer for causes you believe in

This list could go on indefinitely. The important thing is for you to continually expand and improve your sober life. If you do this, you will find that life in recovery can be incredibly enjoyable and rewarding. Yes, you may occasionally miss the intense dopamine rush of sexual acting out, but in time you will learn to truly appreciate the "slow dopamine drip" of healthy pleasures—socializing with friends, providing real support to people you care about, developing a hobby, etc. Rather than compulsively seeking an addictive life filled with gigantic ups and downs, you will find yourself enjoying the relative peace and serenity that your sexual sobriety provides. You will move from shame to grace.

Now is a great time to review the outer boundary of your sexual sobriety plan (Exercise 4), adding more activities that you enjoy to the list of mostly recovery-oriented items that you've likely got. To get started, list five new goals for your life in sexual sobriety.

Example: *I want to have friends that I enjoy being around, who enjoy being around me in return.*

_____

_____

_____

_____

_____

Now, based on the above goals, list five new outer boundary activities, and then add them to your sexual sobriety plan.

Example: *I will go to lunch or dinner with a friend at least once per week.*

_____

_____

_____

_____

_____

Afterword

Hopefully, the exercises in this workbook have given you an in-depth understanding of your addictive process, including the behaviors you need to eliminate, what your underlying issues are, how to avoid relapse, and how to live a happier and healthier life. If you gave honest answers to the exercises herein and fully performed the assigned tasks—in particular the creation of your sexual boundary plan and your portable toolkit—then you have made a great start on lasting recovery and ongoing sexual health.

My sincere hope is that as you completed the exercises you were able to share your work with people who understand sexual addiction and support your recovery—therapists, 12-step sponsors, friends in recovery, trusted clergy, and the like—and that these individuals were able to provide you with a sounding board, feedback, and emotional support when needed. If you have kept your work entirely (or mostly) to yourself, I urge you to rethink this tactic. In the sexual addiction treatment field we have a saying: "Nobody recovers alone." So please reach out to others and ask for help.

Of course, your healing journey is not over simply because you completed this workbook and shared your work with others. In fact, it is only getting started. And that is a wonderful thing. Life in recovery is an adventure, and when you're not actively acting out in your sexual addiction the adventure can be incredibly fun and rewarding. As you move forward with your life, always remember that hope is like the sun, which, as we journey toward it, casts the shadow of our burden behind us.

Live hopeful, live sober, live without shame.

—Robert Weiss LCSW, CSAT-S

Basic Resources for Sexual Addicts

<u>Twelve-Step Groups</u>
- Sex Addicts Anonymous (SAA), 800-477-8191; 713-869-4902, saa-recovery.org/
- Sex and Love Addicts Anonymous (SLAA), 210-828-7900, slaafws.org/
- Sexaholics Anonymous (SA), 866-424-8777, sa.org/
- Sexual Compulsives Anonymous (SCA), 800-977-HEAL, sca-recovery.org/
- Sexual Recovery Anonymous (SRA), sexualrecovery.org/

<u>General Information</u>
- The American Association of Sexuality Educators, Counselors, and Therapists website (aasect.org) offers a great deal of useful information for cybersex addicts.
- The Association for the Treatment of Sexual Abusers website (atsa.com) offers useful information about sexual abuse.
- The Ben Franklin Institute offers, live, online and DVD trainings that can be accessed via their website (bfisummit.com). Much of author Rob Weiss's material has been recorded by them and is available for purchase.
- The International Institute for Trauma & Addiction Professionals (iitap.com) has contact information for therapists, listed by state, who are certified as CSATs (Certified Sex Addiction Therapists).
- Robert Weiss's website (robertweissmsw.com) has extensive information about dealing with and healing from sexual addiction, love addiction, and other intimacy disorders.
- The Safer Society Foundation website (safersociety.org) offers useful information on sexual abuse.
- Dr. Patrick Carnes' website (sexhelp.com) offers a great deal of useful information for sex addicts.
- The Society for the Advancement of Sexual Health website (sash.net) provides contact information for knowledgeable therapists, listed by city and state, as well as information about upcoming sex addiction conferences and training events.

<u>Books</u>
- *Sex Addiction 101: A Basic Guide to Healing from Sex, Porn, and Love Addiction* by Robert Weiss

- *Always Turned On: Sex Addiction in the Digital Age* by Robert Weiss and Dr. Jennifer Schneider
- *Cruise Control: Understanding Sex Addiction in Gay Men (2nd edition)* by Robert Weiss
- *Answers in the Heart: Daily Meditations for Men and Women Recovering from Sex Addiction* (Anonymous)
- *Sex Addicts Anonymous* (Anonymous)
- *Sex and Love Addicts Anonymous* (Anonymous)
- *Contrary to Love: Helping the Sexual Addict* by Dr. Patrick Carnes
- *Don't Call It Love: Recovery from Sex Addiction* by Dr. Patrick Carnes
- *Out of the Shadows: Understanding Sex Addiction* by Dr. Patrick Carnes
- *Breaking the Cycle: Free Yourself from Sex Addiction, Porn Obsession, and Shame* by George Collins and Andrew Adelman
- *No Stones: Women Redeemed from Sexual Addiction* by Marnie Ferree
- *Understanding and Treating Sex Addiction: A Comprehensive Guide for People Who Struggle With Sex Addiction and Those Who Want to Help Them* by Paula Hall

About the Author

Robert Weiss is Senior Vice President of National Clinical Development for Elements Behavioral Health, creating and overseeing addiction and mental health treatment programs for more than a dozen high-end treatment facilities, including Promises Treatment Centers in Malibu, The Ranch in rural Tennessee, and The Right Step in Texas. An internationally acknowledged clinician, he has served as a subject expert on the intersection of human intimacy and digital technology for multiple media outlets including The Oprah Winfrey Network, The New York Times, The Los Angeles Times, The Daily Beast, and CNN, among many others. He is the author of several highly regarded books, including *Sex Addiction 101: A Basic Guide to Healing from Sex, Love, and Porn Addiction,* and *Cruise Control: Understanding Sex Addiction in Gay Men.* He is also a co-author, with Dr. Jennifer Schneider, of *Closer Together, Further Apart* and *Always Turned On: Sex Addiction in the Digital Age.* He writes regularly for Psychology Today, Huffington Post, Psych Central, Counselor Magazine, I Love Recovery Café, Mind Body Green, and Addiction.com, among others. For more information please visit his website, robertweissmsw.com, or follow him on Twitter, @RobWeissMSW.

Other Books by Robert Weiss

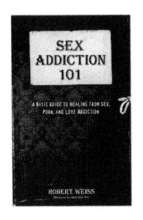

CPSIA information can be obtained
at www.ICGtesting.com
Printed in the USA
LVOW03s2319261116
514605LV00003B/47/P